Windows Powershell and Scripting Made Easy For Sysadmins

A Comprehensive Beginners Guide To Windows Powershell And Scripting To Automate Tasks And Environment

Introduction

Welcome to this PowerShell and Scripting guidebook that focuses on helping Sysadmins learn how to use PowerShell for task Automation and more.

Before we get started:

About this book

This book is for IT professionals, system administrators, DevOps engineers, and IT enthusiasts who are tired of clicking and using the same, lengthy procedures to perform repetitive tasks.

Whether you are working on automating basic tasks, setting up new server environments, automated testing, continuous integration, or continuous development, this book has something for you!

However:

You don't necessarily have to be in the software development field to learn PowerShell scripting.

The content in this book will also be effective for Microsoft users who want to automate their tasks.

Additionally:

You should note that this is not a reference book, nor does it not offer textbook material. We shall be using real-world scenarios on how to use and master PowerShell.

Thus, if you are looking for a reference book or textbook-like material, this book might not be ideal for you.

About this book's structure

The book has various sections, with each section building upon the previous one.

We will start with:

1. Setting up the latest version of PowerShell (ISE), then,

2. Move to the fundamentals of PowerShell scripting language such as Data Types, Objects, and more, and then

3. Talk about PowerShell commands and finish off with scripting

Also worth noting is that this book targets those new to PowerShell scripting.

If you are an experienced PowerShell user, you may not find this book overly helpful.

However, if you're a PowerShell scripting beginner, the strategies, hacks, and tips you shall learn in this book will prove immensely helpful as you embark on an exciting journey of automation with PowerShell.

Let us begin:

Table of Content

Section 1

Introduction to PowerShell

Before we dive into learning how to use PowerShell scripting for automation, let us begin by learning what it is and what it does.

Microsoft PowerShell 101

Microsoft PowerShell is a scripting language used for universal automation, task configuration, and development.

Developed by Microsoft Corporation in 2006, PowerShell has developed exponentially. At the time of this writing, the latest release is PowerShell 7.0.3.

You can read the documentation from the resource page below:

https://linkfy.to/e8pze

Microsoft developed PowerShell as a bridge between scripting, task automation, and operations personnel. Its primary intent was to allow users to automate tasks without having to learn computer programming languages. That makes PowerShell a useful tool for system administrators who do not have a software development background.

Although Microsoft initially released PowerShell for Windows system, it has become open-source, cross-platform, and a powerful scripting language used in large data centers and by local PC users.

Before discussing advanced topics like learning how to write scripts, let us begin by learning the PowerShell scripting language core fundamentals.

We will begin by learning how to set up a PowerShell environment on Windows, Linux, and macOS.

NOTE: If you're using Windows 7—and above—you only need to check whether you have PowerShell already installed.

How to Install Microsoft PowerShell On Windows

The term PowerShell refers to two main things.

1. The first thing is the command-line shell already installed on recent versions of Windows. It is also available in Linux and macOS using the PowerShell core system.

2. The other refers to a scripting language used to combine commands executed by the shell.

The shell and scripting language make up the PowerShell framework we shall be learning how to use in this book.

As mentioned, PowerShell comes pre-installed on the most recent versions of Windows. Although PowerShell has undergone rapid development and bug fixes over the years, the scripts in this book will work whether you are running PowerShell version 2.0 or version 7.0.

That mentioned, if you don't have PowerShell installed on your Windows system, here's how to do it:

Open your browser and navigate to the following resource page:

https:linkfy.to/pMkxl

Next, locate the Windows .msi installer for your System and download it. Once downloaded, launch the installer and follow the installation wizard to complete the installation.

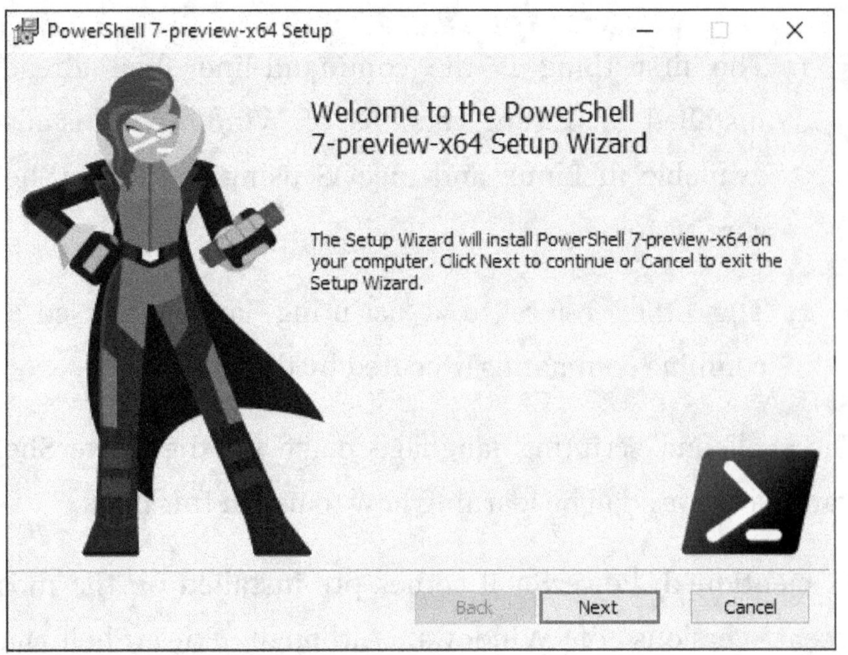

During the installation process, enable the "Enable PowerShell remoting" option. You can also enable and disable other features during installation.

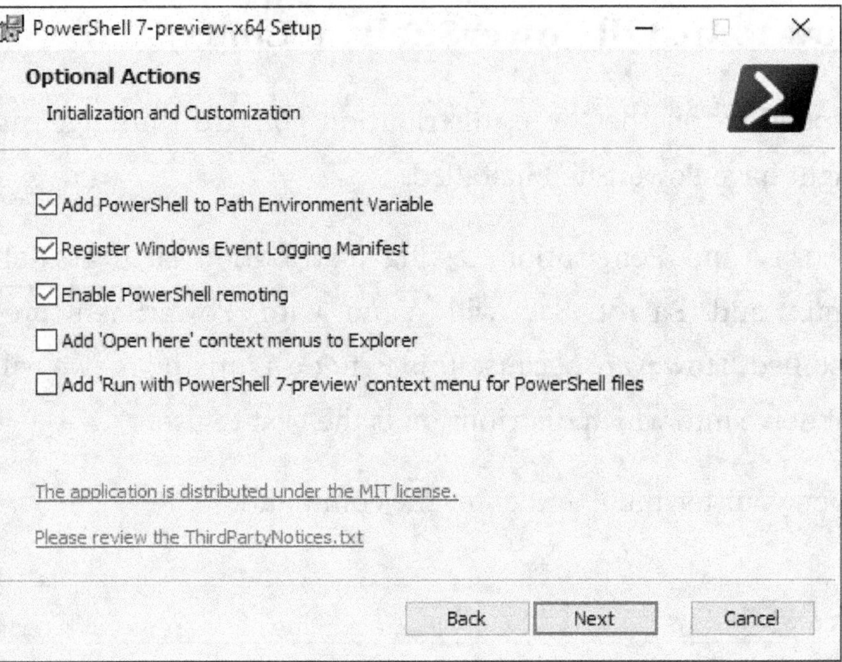

Once done following the prompts, you'll have Windows PowerShell installed on your System:

How to Install PowerShell on Linux

Depending on the Linux distribution you are running, you might have PowerShell installed.

Security and Penetration testing distribution such as Kali Linux and Parrot Sec will come with PowerShell pre-installed. However, because this is not a Linux book, we will not delve into which distribution is the best to use.

Open your terminal and enter the command:

```
wget
https:#github.com/PowerShell/PowerShell/releases/download/v7.0.3/powershell-lts_7.0.3-1.debian.10_amd64.deb
&& sudo dpkg -i powershell-lts_7.0.3-
1.debian.10_amd64.deb
```

If you are running a non-Debian-derived system, open your browser and navigate to the following resource page:

https:linkfy.to/pMkxl

Once there, download the installer for your System.

Once the installation completes, launch PowerShell using the command `pwsh`. Depending on your system configuration, you may need superuser privileges.

How to Install PowerShell on macOS

For macOS users, you can get the latest PowerShell installer on the official GitHub release page.

Open the browser and navigate to this resource page:

https:linkfy.to/pMkxl

Once there, download the pkg installer. Once downloaded, launch the installer and follow the instructions.

Launching the PowerShell Console

Once you have PowerShell installed on your System, you can launch the console from either the start menu for Windows users, terminal for Linux users, and Applications menu for macOS.

Upon launch, you should get a console with a flashing cursor, as shown in the image below:

Once PowerShell is up and running, you will get a *prompt* indicator showing that the shell is ready to accept commands.

The PowerShell prompt is indicated by the PS, followed by the current System path. If you run as a regular user, the path will be in your home directory. If you run as an administrator, the path will be `C:\Windows\System32`.

In PowerShell, we can start exploring the commands available. If you are a *cmd* user, you can execute similar PowerShell commands such as `dir`, `cd`, `mkdir`, etc.

Under the hood, the DOS "commands" are not commands in PowerShell, but aliases or pseudonyms translated from DOS commands to commands that PowerShell understands.

Let us test out some commands:

In the current PowerShell workspaces, execute the command `cd` to change directory or `dir` to list content in the current directory.

```
PS C:\Windows\system32> dir

Directory: C:\Windows\system32

Mode                 LastWriteTime         Length Name
----                 -------------         ------ ----

d------        12/7/2019  12:49 PM                0409
d------         9/9/2020  10:19 AM
AdvancedInstallers
d------        12/7/2019  12:14 PM                am-et
```

```
d------          12/7/2019 12:14 PM
AppLocker

-----------------output truncated----------------------
---------------
```

In PowerShell, you can use the TAB key to autocomplete a command. For example, if you type the command GET, followed by the TAB key, it will list all the commands you can execute. We will discuss more PowerShell commands in later sections of this book.

You can explore other cmd commands to see whether they work in PowerShell. However, this is not crucial as PowerShell has its own set of commands that we shall discuss next:

Section 2
PowerShell Commands

Like all other programming languages, PowerShell has a unique set of built-in commands understood by PowerShell only.

We can define commands as a set of executable expressions from a single executable file such as `diskpart.exe` to commands such as `Clear-Host`, `Get-Alias`, and more.

PowerShell also allows us to write personal commands. However, if you run a command that PowerShell does not understand, you will get an error:

```
PS C:\Windows\system32\WindowsPowerShell> unknown

unknown: The term 'unknown' is not recognized as the
name of a cmdlet, function, script file, or operable
program. Check the spelling of the name, or if a path
was included, verify that the

path is correct and try again.

At line:1 char:1

+ unknown

+ ~~~~~~~

    + CategoryInfo          : ObjectNotFound:
(unknown:String) [], CommandNotFoundException

    + FullyQualifiedErrorId : CommandNotFoundException
```

To get a list of all commands included in PowerShell by default, use the command `Get-Command`. That will give you the command type, name of the command, version, and the source:

```
PS C:\Windows\system32\WindowsPowerShell> Get-Command

CommandType        Name                    Version      Source

-----------        ----                    -------      ------

Alias              Add-AppPackage 2.0.1.0       Appx

Alias              Add-AppPackageVolume 2.0.1.0     Appx

Alias              Add-AppProvisionedPackage 3.0
Dism

Alias              Add-ProvisionedAppPackage 3.0
Dism

Alias              Add-ProvisionedAppxPackage 3.0
Dism

-------------------------output truncated----------------------
```

If you look closely at all PowerShell-recognized commands, you will notice that they follow a similar pattern Verb-Noun.

The purpose of this common PowerShell characteristic is to make the language as intuitive and as simple to use as possible. Although you don't have to follow naming convention when creating custom commands, it is best to do so, especially when building mass-distribution tools.

PowerShell has four main types of Command types:

1. **An Alias:** Aliases are pseudonyms for DOS commands. For example, a command like `clear`, used to clear the terminal, is an alias of `Clear-Host`.

2. **Cmdlets:** cmdlets are commands executed in a PowerShell environment. We can also define a cmdlet as a lightweight command written in other programming languages and used in the PowerShell environment, often called using the PowerShell API.

3. **Functions:** Functions are also another type of PowerShell commands. Functions are written natively in PowerShell scripting languages and used to perform specific tasks.

4. **Scripts:** The other type of commands you will encounter in PowerShell are external commands written by either you or other users.

You will often interact with cmdlets and Functions when programming in PowerShell.

In PowerShell, most—if not all—commands support parameters, which are values or options passed to modify how the commands work.

For example:

A command such as `Get-Command` supports parameters that allow you to list only specific command types. For example, to get commands that only use the *verb* Remove, use the command: `Get-Command -Verb Remove`

```
PS C:\Windows\system32\WindowsPowerShell> Get-Command
-Verb Remove

CommandType        Name
Version     Source


-----------        ----

-------     ------

Alias              Remove-ProvisioningPackage
3.0         Provisioning

Alias              Remove-TrustedProvisioningCertificate
3.0         Provisioning

Function           Remove-AutologgerConfig
1.0.0.0     EventTracingManagement

Function           Remove-BCDataCacheExtension
1.0.0.0     BranchCache
```

Types of verbs used in the PowerShell language include Get, Set, Update, Enable, Remove, etc. Due to the PowerShell's intuitive nature, the commands perform actions according to their verbs.

Documentation and Help

PowerShell is a useful tool because it integrates all its documentation in the language.

Here, we will discuss how to get command help, view, and update the documentation.

To get a command's documentation in PowerShell, we use the command `help` or `Get-Help`, similar to the man command in Linux.

The `Get-Help` command displays the documentation in a standardized way: SYNOPSIS, SYNTAX, DESCRIPTION, RELATED LINKS, and REMARKS.

Each of these sections allows you to find out what the command does and where you can get more information about it if you need to.

Here's an example:

```
PS C:\Users\salem> Get-Help Get-Command

NAME

    Get-Command

SYNTAX

    Get-Command [[-ArgumentList] <Object[]>] [-Verb
<string[]>] [-Noun <string[]>] [-Module <string[]>] [-
FullyQualifiedModule <ModuleSpecification[]>] [-
TotalCount <int>] [-Syntax]

ALIASES

    gcm

REMARKS

    Get-Help cannot find the Help files for this
cmdlet on this computer. It is displaying only partial
help.

        -- To download and install Help files for the
module that includes this cmdlet, use Update-Help.

        -- To view the Help topic for this cmdlet
online, type: "Get-Help Get-Command -Online" or

            go to
https:#go.microsoft.com/fwlink/?LinkID=113309.
```

Like all commands, the `Get-Help` command supports various arguments. Although passing the `Get-Help` command without arguments can be extremely helpful, using it with arguments such as -Examples customizes the output and the help returned. The -Examples parameter provides real-world use cases of the requested command. For example:

```
Get-Help Wait-Process -Examples

--------------- Example 1: Stop a process and wait ----
----------

    PS C:\> $nid = (Get-Process notepad).id

    PS C:\> Stop-Process -Id $nid

    PS C:\> Wait-Process -Id $nid
```

This example stops the Notepad process, then waits until the process stops before it continues with the next command.

The first command makes use of the Get-Process cmdlet for getting the Notepad process ID. It stores the ID in the $nid variable.

Next, the second command makes use of Stop-Process cmdlet for stopping the process with the ID stored in $nid.

Finally, the third command makes use of Wait-Process to wait for the Notepad process to stop. Wait-Process is the ID parameter used to identify the process.

```
--------------- Example 2: Specifying a process --
-----------

    PS C:\> $p = Get-Process notepad

    PS C:\> Wait-Process -Id $p.id

    PS C:\> Wait-Process -Name "notepad"

    PS C:\> Wait-Process -InputObject $p
```

You can also get more information about a command using the Get-Help command and other arguments such as Detailed and Full parameters, which give you a complete rundown of what that command does.

About General Topics

Besides having detailed documentation about individual commands, PowerShell also has helpful documentation for broader subjects called *About Topics.*

The About Topics are snippets containing help about large topics or specific command, for example, a topic such as PowerShell core commands in the documentation.

To view documentation for a particular topic., use the command Get-help <topic_name>. Here's an example:

```
PS C:\Users\salem> Get-Help about_remote_jobs

ABOUT REMOTE JOBS

SHORT DESCRIPTION

Describes how to run background jobs on remote
computers.

DETAILED DESCRIPTION

A background job is a command that runs asynchronously
without interacting

with the current session. The command prompt returns
immediately, and you

can continue to use the session while the job runs.

-------------------------output truncated----------------
```

You can get all the topics available in PowerShell using the asterisk (*) wildcard in the Get-Help command's name parameter.

For example:

```
PS C:\Users\salem> Get-help -Name about*


Name                              Category  Module
Synopsis
----                              --------  ------
--------


    about_Aliases                         HelpFile
    about_Alias_Provider                  HelpFile
    about_Arithmetic_Operators            HelpFile
    about_Arrays                          HelpFile
    about_Assignment_Operators            HelpFile
    about_Automatic_Variables             HelpFile
    about_Break                           HelpFile
    about_Calculated_Properties           HelpFile
    about_Certificate_Provider            HelpFile

---------------OUTPUT TRUNCATED----------------------
```

Applying the asterisk (*) to a PowerShell command asks the shell to search all possible topics containing "about."

Because there's more than one command, PowerShell will display a list of the topics, allowing you to view them all at once. You can then use an *About Topic* individually to get detailed information, as shown in the previous section.

Updating PowerShell Documentation

The PowerShell documentation system is an incredible tool for users who want to learn more about a particular command and various topics.

One of the great features of the PowerShell documentation is that it's dynamic. That means the documentation grows and gets updated when the development team applies new features, releases, and bug fixes.

PowerShell provides a way for users to sync their documentation to the current version using the `Update-Help` command. This command allows PowerShell cmdlets and functions to point to a specific internet URL to pull the latest documentation into the host system. `Update-Help` can also work for functions and tools created by other PowerShell users, not just the built-in ones.

PowerShell provides useful tools developers can use to write documentation to their tools but still retain a copy of the repository containing the current documentation.

You may also get errors when running the `Update-Help` command as the documentations' locations may be down or migrated to a new URL. Hence, the Update-Help command may not always provide the latest documentation version.

To update your PowerShell documentation to the latest version, ensure you are running the latest PowerShell version—discussed in the installation section—and as an Administrator:

```
PS C:\Users\salem> Update-help

Remove-Job


Updating Help for module CimCmdlets


Updating Help for module CimCmdlets
Locating Help Content...
[ooooooooooooooooooooooooooooooooooooooooooooooooooooooooo
ooooooooooooooooooooooooooooooooooooooooooooooooooooooooo
ooooooooooooooooooooooooooooooooooooooooooooooooooooooooo
oooooooooooooooooooo]
Exit-PSSession
```

<u>Summary</u>

This chapter has discussed basic PowerShell commands that will help you get started with PowerShell scripting and automation.

As with everything new, you may not know what you do not know; thus, all you can do is get started and figure out the rest as you go along. That's why the `Get-command` command is powerful: it helps you discover what PowerShell offers.

Let us continue the PowerShell journey:

Section 3

PowerShell Scripting Core Concepts

This section discusses the basics of the PowerShell scripting language.

Among other things, we shall discuss the most fundamental concepts in all programming languages, including variables, data types, objects, data structures, loops, and more.

Worth noting is that although these concepts are foundational in all programming languages, PowerShell presents them differently.

If you have ever heard a PowerShell super user say, *"Everything in PowerShell is an Object,"* this section will help you discover what that means.

Let's start:

Variables

If you have prior programming knowledge, you will be familiar with the term *variable*.

We can define a variable as a value stored in a computer program where its value changes based on the conditions offered by the running namespace and the information provided to the program. Simplified, we can say that we use a variable to store a value.

You can think of a variable as a storage box where you store values you require more than once. Hence, instead of buying items every time you need it, you can get it from the storage unit. The good thing about the storage unit—*variable*—is that it can change, allowing you to add and remove items to it as you see fit.

The variability of a variable makes it possible for developers to build dynamic code that can adapt to various program changes instead of a single-use case.

Here's how to work with variables in PowerShell:

How to Declare PowerShell Variables

Variable declaration is the process a program uses to tell the computer it needs space to store some data. You can learn more about it from the resource page below:

https://linkfy.to/3ECr9

When declaring a variable, you start with a dollar sign ($) followed by the variable's name. Doing that tells PowerShell you want to call a variable, not a function, cmdlet, or an executable otherwise, you will get an error.

For example, declare a variable to store the number of logins:

```
PS C:\Users\salem> $logins = 10;
```

Do not worry about what the equal sign means at the moment. We will get to that later:

From the above command, we have created a variable and stored a value in it. PowerShell also has built-in variables— also called *automatic variables*—that you can call using the $<variable name> as shown below:

```
PS C:\Users\salem> $host

Name             : ConsoleHost

Version          : 7.1.0-rc.2

InstanceId       : 427682d7-7563-42bd-b41a-
ef51dfb4da63

UI               :
System.Management.Automation.Internal.Host.InternalHos
tUserInterface

CurrentCulture   : en-US

CurrentUICulture : en-US

PrivateData      :
Microsoft.PowerShell.ConsoleHost+ConsoleColorProxy

DebuggerEnabled  : True

IsRunspacePushed : False

Runspace         :
System.Management.Automation.Runspaces.LocalRunspace
```

To view information about PowerShell built-in variables, use the command:

```
PS C:\Users\salem> Get-Help about_Automatic_variables
```

You can learn more automatic variables from the resource page below:

https:linkfy.to/oHMsK

Apart from built-in variables, PowerShell supports user-defined variables ($login) created by the user.

User-Defined Variables

Most programming languages demand that you declare a variable—it must exist—before you can use it. We have already seen the variable declaration process above, where we pass the variable's name and value:

```
$login = 10; {Variable name and Value respectively}
```

If you call a variable that does not exist—meaning a variable not declared by the user or built-in—you will get an InvalidOperation error. For example:

```
PS C:\Users\salem> $DoesNotExist

InvalidOperation: The variable' $DoesNotExist'
cannot be retrieved because it has not been set.
```

However, depending on the configuration you've set for your PowerShell instance, you may not get any error. You can enable strict mode using the command:

```
PS C:\Users\salem> Set-strictmode -version latest
```

PowerShell script mode forces PowerShell to display errors when set PowerShell programming practices get violated. For example, it returns an error when you call an undeclared variable. It's good to turn on strict mode, especially when experimenting with PowerShell.

You can get more information about the command use case:

```
PS C:\Users\salem> Get-Help Set-Strictmode
```

Once you have a variable declared and initialized—the process of assigning a value to the variable—you can reference it using its name.

NOTE: Although variables are dynamically changeable, the variable initialized value does not change unless someone explicitly changes it or a namespace in the program changes the value. We shall discuss more details about namespaces in later parts of this book.

Another way to declare a variable is to use the `Set-Variable` command. This command accepts two main arguments:

1. Name – the name of the variable

2. Value – the value to assign to the declared variable

For example:

```
PS C:\Users\salem> Set-Variable -Name login -Value 10
PS C:\Users\salem> Get-Variable -Name login
```

```
Name                            Value
----                            -----
login                           10
```

******* Basically, the syntax $<variable name> = <variable value> is a shorter way for declaring and initializing a variable instead of using the Set-Variable command.

You can list all available variables stored in the memory by using the Get-Variable command without arguments:

```
PS C:\Users\salem> Get-Variable
Name                            Value
----                            -----

?                               True
^                               Get-Variable
$                               login
args                            {}
ConfirmPreference               High
DebugPreference                 SilentlyContinue
EnabledExperimentalFeatures     {}
-----------------output truncated--------------------
```

Automatic Variables

In the above subsection, we briefly discussed automatic variables built-in to PowerShell. Automatic variables are premade and used by PowerShell for configuration and functionality. It is good to note that automatic variables are changeable but doing so is not ideal—you should treat them as *read-only*.

Let us discuss some of the important automatic variables you are likely to encounter while working with PowerShell.

1: The $$ variable

The $$ variable —often pronounced as the dollar-dollar sign command—fetches the last token or command in the last line accepted by the current PowerShell session.

It acts as a history command that gets the last executed command in the PowerShell session. That means if you close PowerShell, re-launch it, then use the $$ variable, you won't get any results. For example:

```
PS C:\Users\salem> $$
```

```
Get-Variable
```

A new session of PowerShell will be empty.

```
PS C:\Users\salem> $$
```

```
PS C:\Users\salem>
```

It's good to note that the command's output may vary depending on the command you executed last.

2: The $Event Variable

The Event variable represents an event under processing contained in the `PSEventArgs` Class. This variable's population only happens within an event's registration Action block, such as `Register-ObjectEvent`.

The variable's value is similar to the object returned by the `Get-Event` cmdlet. That means you can use the Event variable properties, such as `$Event.TimeGenerated`, in an Action script block.

You can learn more about this from these resources pages:

https:linkfy.to/Mstn2

https:linkfy.to/iBpHn

3: The $null variable

Another fun variable in PowerShell is the `null` variable used to hold nothing. This variable is useful when you want to create a non-value assigned variable.

For example:

If you have a variable $login and you want to declare it, you have to provide a value; otherwise, PowerShell will return an error. However, this can be a problem, especially when you want to assign an empty value to a variable.

You can solve this by assigning the variable to $null:

```
PS C:\Users\salem> $login = $null

PS C:\Users\salem> $login

PS C:\Users\salem> $DoesNotExist

InvalidOperation: The variable' $DoesNotExist'
cannot be retrieved because it has not been set.
```

As you can see, once we assign $null to $login variable, it does not return an error because PowerShell perceives it as already declared and assigned compared to the $DoesNotExist variable.

In reality, the variable $login contains an empty value—shown below:

```
PS C:\Users\salem> Get-Variable -Name login


Name                          Value

----                          -----

login
```

The `$null` variable may seem useless right now, but it is essential, especially when you're working with functions and debugging your code.

4: The $LASTEXITCODE variable

Now that we're speaking of code debugging, another useful command for this is the `$LASTEXITCODE` variable, used to return the `return value` once an external program executes.

Normally, once you run a program and exit it, it returns a value—called a *return* or *exit code*. This code indicates a message such as "Successful, Error, or another type of message. Zero *return value* indicates success, and 1 indicates an error or other type of message.

If you are familiar with programming in languages such as C++, you may have seen a format such as:

```
#include <stdio>

using namespace std;


int main() {

    cout << "Hello, world!" << endl;

    return 0;

}
```

This format indicates a successfully-executed program.

When you run a PowerShell program, you can view the exit code once the program completes executing. By default, the exit code is hidden, and programs only show the user the expected output. However, using this variable, you can view the exit code returned by a program.

For example, consider the ping tool—ping.exe located in C:\Windows\System32). If you ping a valid domain and use the $LASTEXITCODE variable, you will see it executes successfully with exit code 0. However, an invalid domain will return an exit code 1.

```
PS C:\Users\salem> ping google.com

Pinging google.com [216.58.223.110] with 32 bytes of
data:

Reply from 216.58.223.110: bytes=32 time=29ms TTL=57

Reply from 216.58.223.110: bytes=32 time=21ms TTL=57

Reply from 216.58.223.110: bytes=32 time=19ms TTL=57

Reply from 216.58.223.110: bytes=32 time=19ms TTL=57


Ping statistics for 216.58.223.110:

    Packets: Sent = 4, Received = 4, Lost = 0 (0%
loss),

Approximate round trip times in milli-seconds:

    Minimum = 19ms, Maximum = 29ms, Average = 22ms

PS C:\Users\salem> $LASTEXITCODE

0

PS C:\Users\salem> ping domaininvalid.io

Ping request could not find host domaininvalid.io.
Please check the name and try again.

PS C:\Users\salem> $LASTEXITCODE


1

PS C:\Users\salem>
```

That comes in handy when debugging what is working and what causes errors.

5: Preference Variables

Preference variables are another type of automatic variables supported by PowerShell. Their primary use it to control the default configuration of various output streams such as `Error, Verbose, Warning, Information, Progress,` **and** `Debug`

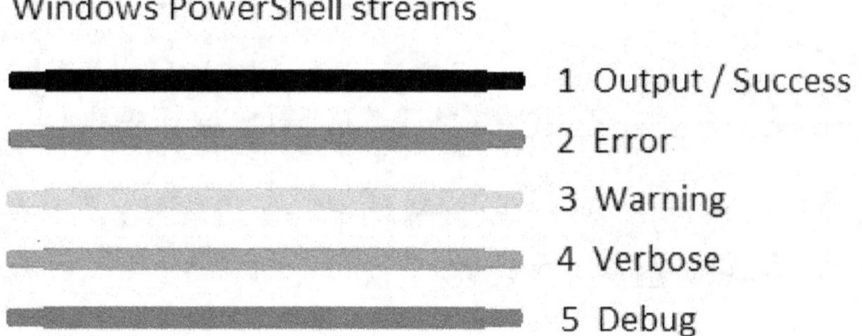

PowerShell Output Streams

Output streams or redirection redirect output in PowerShell. By default, the output gets redirected to the console but can also get altered to redirect to a specific output stream or even file types—we'll discuss redirection a bit more in upcoming sections.

PowerShell has five main types of output streams. Do not get confused; you will understand them better once you master PowerShell.

1. **The Success stream:** This is the default stream for successful results. You can use the `Write-Output` cmdlet to redirect output to this stream. For example:

```
PS C:\Users\salem> $example = Write-Output -Messsage
"Example Redirection"

PS C:\Users\salem> $example

-Messsage
```

2. **Error stream:** The error stream handles error conditions. When you see a red screaming message when you execute the wrong command, that's the error stream handling things. The errors for this output stream also get added to the $Errors variable. This variable can also allow you to view errors that

occur in your script. To use the error stream explicitly, use the `Write-Error` cmdlet. Consider an error output stream shown below:

```
PS C:\Users\salem> $myerror = Write-Error -Message "I
am handled by error stream"

Write-Error: I am handled by error stream
```

By default, i.e., without using the error stream, the variable `$myerror` acts like any standard variable. However, once we explicitly pass it to the error stream, it displays as an error.

3. **Warning stream:** The warning stream is similar to the error output stream but intended for error conditions considered less severe than those in the error stream. Their main indicator is a less-screaming light yellow color. You specify this output stream using the `Write-Warning` cmdlet. Unlike the error output stream, warnings don't get stored in a variable. Here's an example of warning output redirection:

```
PS C:\Users\salem> $warnme = Write-Warning -Message
"I am a handled by warning stream"

WARNING: I am a handled by warning stream
```

4. **Verbose Stream**: The verbose output stream is for messages that help users troubleshoot their commands or scripts. To specify the verbose stream explicitly, use the `Write-Verbose` cmdlet. Most commands support the verbose output stream by default and are callable using the syntax:

```
<command name> -Verbose parameter.

PS C:\Users\salem> $meVerbose = Write-Verbose -Message
"I am handled by Verbose stream" -Verbose

VERBOSE: I am handled by Verbose stream
```

5. **Information stream:** As the name suggests, the information stream is for messages that help users understand what their scripts are doing—you can consider it similar to a log output stream. It is also common to use this output stream to deliver information to PowerShell. To specify the information output stream, we use the Write-Information cmdlet. Consider the example below:

```
PS C:\Users\salem> $info = Write-Information -
MessageData "I am handled by Information stream" -
InformationAction Continue

I am handled by Information stream
```

6. **Debug stream:** As usual, the debug stream helps debug PowerShell scripts. Its primary use is helping scripters understand why the code fails or result in a certain error. To write to this stream explicitly, use the Write-Debug cmdlet. Consider the example shown below:

```
PS C:\Users\salem> $DebugPreference = "Continue"

PS C:\Users\salem> $debugme = Write-Debug "I am
handled by Debug stream"

DEBUG: I am handled by Debug stream
```

The first command sets the $DebugPreference to "continue" displaying the message to the console, which is by default set to "SilentlyContinue" without displaying the message.

7. **Progress stream:** This output stream displays messages that display the progress of no longer running scripts and commands. Use the Write-Progress cmdlet to specify this stream explicitly. The progress stream does not support redirection. Do not worry about what the command below does, but a Write progress stream would look like this:

```
for ($i = 1; $i -le 100; $i++ )

   {

       Write-Progress -Activity "Search in Progress"
 -Status "$i% Complete:" -PercentComplete $i;

   }
```

We will learn what the code above does in upcoming sections. If any of the information provided above seems confusing, please remember that you shall cultivate a deeper understanding as we delve deeper into PowerShell.

External Resources

Here's a list of prepared resources you can use to understand more about output streams and variables. Also, consider using the Get-Help command to learn more.

https:linkfy.to/UhvhX

https:linkfy.to/td4J8

https:linkfy.to/IWLc6

https:linkfy.to/LcQDP

Naming Variables

Beginner programmers often receive this advice from seasoned ones: *"A name does not convey an individual's meaning or story."* That is very sound advice; it means just because a variable has a name does not mean it's the right one.

Variable naming is something you should master because it makes the code much easier to understand. Nothing is as frustrating as leaving your computer desk only to come back a few hours later, only to struggle to remember what your code means.

You should always give your variables a name that's not too long but conveys the variable's meaning. For example, you can use the following names to represent the computer's name. Which is better?

```
$pn = $env:computername
```

```
$pc_name = $env:computername
```

Remember that both are valid in PowerShell, but the first one does not say what it does. Hence, you should find meaningful and short variable names. Apart from meaningful names, variable names should:

- Always have a preceding dollar sign ($)

- Only contain letters, numbers, and underscores

- Not use the name of a pre-defined variable, cmdlet, or function

- Enclose other characters in curly braces:

```
- ${myname@@} = "PowerShell"
```

Let's now discuss PowerShell Data types:

PowerShell Data Types

Data types are another important programming concept. Data types help describe or define the storage of a variable.

PowerShell data types can seem confusing, especially if you have never programmed before. They are also massive, and discussing each one of them is beyond the scope of this book.

Nevertheless, in this subsection, we shall endeavor to discuss them in an easy-to-understand manner. However, PowerShell does not require you to specify the data type of your variable explicitly. It automatically chooses the data type upon initialization, which can cause problems at times.

Let us begin:

PowerShell utilizes the Microsoft .NET Framework data types. These data types supported by PowerShell include:

- `[Int][Int32]`
- `[long]`
- `[decimal]`
- `[single]`
- `[double]`
- `[byte]`
- `[char]`
- `[string]`
- `[DateTime]`
- `[array]`
- `[xml]`
- `[hashtable]`
- `[guid]`
- `[ScriptBlock]`

Let us tackle the most crucial and beginner-friendly data types.

NOTE: Because they're a bit more advanced and this is a beginner-friendly book, we won't discuss data types like `[xml]`, `[guid]`, **and** `[ScriptBlock]`.

[Int][Int32] : 32-bit Signed Integer

The first PowerShell data type we shall discuss is the *integrals or Numeric Literals.*

Integrals help represent numerical values. [Int] or [Int32] is 32-bit signed integers found in the .NET framework System.Int32 class. It is the default numeric data type used by PowerShell. To create a 32-bit unsigned integer, we use [uint] or [uint32].

A 32-bit integer value has a limit on the number of data it can store in bytes. To find out the maximum and minimum value a 32-bit integer can use, use the command:

```
PS C:\Users\salem> [int]::MinValue
-2147483648
PS C:\Users\salem> [int]::MaxValue
2147483647
PS C:\Users\salem> [uint]::MinValue
0
PS C:\Users\salem> [uint]::MaxValue
4294967295
```

[Long] : 64-bit signed integer

A [long] and a]ulong] are integral values representing 64-bit signed integer and 64-bit unsigned integer. You will find them in System. Int64 and System. uin64 classes, respectively, of the .NET framework.

Similar to a 32-bit signed and unsigned integer, you can determine the maximum and minimum range of these types:

```
PS C:\Users\salem> [long]::MinValue
-9223372036854775808

  PS C:\Users\salem> [long]::MaxValue
9223372036854775807
PS C:\Users\salem> [ulong]::MinValue
0
PS C:\Users\salem> [ulong]::MaxValue
18446744073709551615
```

[Decimal] : A 128-bit decimal Value

A decimal is a 128-bit decimal value declared in System.Decimal structure of the .NET framework. Decimals can hold both Positive and Negative values. We mainly use them in high accuracy calculations to determine the range of the decimal type as:

```
PS C:\Users\salem> [decimal]::MinValue
```

```
-79228162514264337593543950335
```

```
PS C:\Users\salem> [decimal]::MaxValue
```

```
79228162514264337593543950335
```

The range is mainly expressed as (-7.9 x 1028 to 7.9 x 1028) / (100 to 28).

[single] : Single Precision 32-Bit Floating Point Number

A single data type belongs to a group of data types in PowerShell known as *floating Point* values. We have two main types of floating-point value: Floats or singles and double.

A single or float is a 32-bit Single Precision Floating Point value found in the `System.Single` of the .NET framework class.

Here's how to find out the max and min range value of the single data type:

```
PS C:\Users\salem> [float]::MinValue

-3.402823E+38

PS C:\Users\salem> [float]::MaxValue

3.402823E+38
```

[double] : Double precision 64-bit Floating Point Number

As mentioned, the double belongs to Floating data types. It is an instance of the `System.Double` of the .NET framework class. You can use [double] to specify the double type in PowerShell:

```
PS C:\Users\salem> [double]::minValue

-1.79769313486232E+308

PS C:\Users\salem> [double]::maxValue

1.79769313486232E+308
```

[string] : Fixed Length Unicode Characters

A string is a common type in most programming languages. We often use it to represent a set or string of Unicode characters. We indicate it by surrounding the characters in double quotation marks.

For example: "`Hello`" is a string. We can also regard a set of characters such as "123" as a string. Strings are in the `Sytem.String` class in the .NET framework.

You can learn more about string from the following resource page:

https:linkfy.to/4PkZS

[bool] : Boolean True or False Values

Booleans are fundamental data types in most programming languages. We utilize them to hold binary values, i.e., two main values: True or False values.

Further, we (WE means programmers) usually and mainly combine them with conditional statements to add more functionality to the program. For example:

```
$player1_score = 10;

$player2_score = 40;

$player1_winning = False;
```

The above example shows a simple Booleans use case. However, Boolean values change dynamically within a program.

As mentioned earlier, because this is a beginner-centric book, we won't delve deeper into other advanced data types.

Keep in mind that as your PowerShell skills grow, you will need to expand your knowledge. Here's a list of prepared-resources you can use to enhance your data type knowledge. If you find data types confusing, you can ignore them for now and concentrate on learning as much of PowerShell as you can. Eventually, you'll master working with data types as your skills develop:

https:linkfy.to/wumzY

https:linkfy.to/P51c0

https:linkfy.to/qKUaY

https:linkfy.to/GCuPS

https:linkfy.to/jrVTI

https:linkfy.to/XLoCw

https:linkfy.to/tLSYx

https:linkfy.to/dNQg7

https:linkfy.to/61Ifo

Type Casting

Type Casting is the process of force converting a specific type to another data type. For example, you can force-convert a single to an `int`. We perform Type Casting using the *Casting Operator,* which is the square brackets.

Consider the example below:

```
PS C:\Users\salem> [int]"890"

890
```

In the code above, we converted the string "890" to an integer. You can check the data type in PowerShell by calling the GetType() method.

For example:

```
PS C:\Users\salem> $my_int = [int]"890"
PS C:\Users\salem> $my_int.GetType()


IsPublic IsSerial Name                                     BaseType
-------- -------- ----                                     --------
True     True     Int32                                    System.ValueType
```

As you can see, the variable $my_int gets converted from a string to a [Int32].

Objects

Can you remember the statement, "everything is an *Object* in PowerShell?" Let's expound on that now.

We can refer to an Object as an instance of a specific class or template. You may recall cases where we've mentioned that a certain data type is an instance or found in `System.Double` class, for example.

In this case, the `System.Double` is the class, and double data type is an instance of such as class. This programming paradigm method is what we call Object-Oriented Programming—but that's a story for another day!

Inside a specific class, there exist *methods* which are certain things an object's instance can do. We can also find *Properties* inside a Class, dictating data about a class instance. In short, you can consider Classes as blueprints for a certain object type.

Because this may seem very abstract, let's get out of programming jargon and talk about it using real-world objects.

Consider a car:

If we want to build a blueprint for all cars (car Class), we must define basic data about all types of cars (properties) and the actions every car should be able to perform (methods).

With that information, we can know that:

Every car should have wheels, model number, manufacture date, and such basic information. These are what we call the car's *properties*.

The basic operations every car should perform are ignition, steer in a specified vector, and stop. We can refer to these as the car's methods.

Therefore, using the Car class, we can create a car called myCar and provide all its basic details. Here's an example:

```
myCar = Car(); # create a myCar object using the Car
Class
myCar.wheels = 4; # set the wheel property

myCar.modelNumber = "X76X"; # set the model number
for the myCar object

myCar.manufactureDate = 2012; # set the manufacture
date for myCar object.

myCar.ignite() # call the ignition method


myCar.steer(2.44, 1.58, 3.45, 80deg) # steer the car
in a specific direction
```

If we disregard the code's implementation, we can see that we created a `myCar` object from the basic car template and provided our specified values. The car also ignites and moves in a specific direction, both dictated by the Class methods.

Using Select-Object cmdlet

In PowerShell, we can view an object's properties and methods. To view the properties of an object, use the `Select-Object` commands and the `property` argument. Here's an example:

```
PS C:\Users\salem> Select-Object -InputObject string -
Property *

Length

-------

    6
```

That gives us the properties contained in the String class. To access an object's property directly, use the dot (.) notation followed by the property's name. For example, `string. length`

As you become more familiar with PowerShell scripting, accessing `Object` methods and properties will become easier.

Using Get-Elements cmdlet

Above, we discovered that we could use the `Select-Object` followed by the `property` argument to display an object's properties.

We can also use the `Get-Elements` cmdlet to get an object's properties and methods. This command displays all an object's properties and methods, which we collectively refer to as *Object Members*.

Here's an example:

```
PS C:\Users\salem> $single = 10.5
PS C:\Users\salem> $single | Get-Member

    TypeName: System.Double

Name          MemberType Definition

----          ---------- ----------

CompareTo    Method      int CompareTo(System.Object
value), int CompareTo(double value), int
IComparable.CompareTo(System.Object…

Equals       Method      bool Equals(System.Object obj),
bool Equals(double obj), bool
IEquatable[double].Equals(double other)

GetHashCode Method       int GetHashCode()

GetType      Method      type GetType()
```

```
GetTypeCode Method      System.TypeCode GetTypeCode(),
System.TypeCode IConvertible.GetTypeCode()

ToBoolean    Method       bool
IConvertible.ToBoolean(System.IFormatProvider
provider)

ToByte       Method       byte
IConvertible.ToByte(System.IFormatProvider provider)

ToChar       Method       char
IConvertible.ToChar(System.IFormatProvider provider)

ToDateTime Method        datetime
IConvertible.ToDateTime(System.IFormatProvider
provider)

ToDecimal    Method       decimal
IConvertible.ToDecimal(System.IFormatProvider
provider)

ToDouble     Method       double
IConvertible.ToDouble(System.IFormatProvider provider)

---------------output truncated-----------
```

Boom! That is something.

Once we pipe an object to the Get-Member command, it dumps all the information it can about it. The class manages all the properties and methods of all the objects it instantiates.

Calling Methods of an Object

As mentioned, methods act as actions that an object can perform. For example, a car ignition is an action. To call an object's method, we use the same dot (.) notation we use in properties, but methods use parenthesis.

For example, a method for the int32 object is converting the into to string:

```
PS C:\Users\salem> $single.ToString()

10.5
```

To verify the type has been changed, trying piping it to the Get-Element cmdlet:

```
PS C:\Users\salem> $single.ToString() | Get-Member

   TypeName: System.String

Name                    MemberType                 Definition
----                    ----------                 ----------

Clone                   Method
System.Object Clone(), System.Object
ICloneable.Clone()

CompareTo               Method                          int
CompareTo(System.Object value), int CompareTo(string
```

```
Contains                 Method                    bool
Contains(string value), bool Contains(string value,
System.StringComparison comparisonType), bool
Contains(char value), bool Contains(char val…

CopyTo                   Method                    void
CopyTo(int sourceIndex, char[] destination, int
destinationIndex, int count)

------------------output truncated------------
```

Data Structures

Data structures are special data types used to store multiple data pieces of data. Although they may sound weird, they are data types and thus represented as objects in PowerShell.

There are three main types of data structures:

1. Arrays

2. ArrayLists

3. Hashtables

Before we discuss data structures, it's good to understand that you will not understand them all at once. Only by using them will you master them.

1: Arrays

Arrays are one of the fundamental data structures in PowerShell and most computer programming languages. An array is a list of variables represented by a single variable.

If we consider a single array as a single storage unit, then an array is an assembly of storage units storing related values. For example, an array can include a series of storage units for storing farm equipment.

If you head is spinning a little, let's simplify things a bit more:

Suppose you have a class, a regular class, not an OOP class, of students, and you want to store their scores. You can store this data as:

```
Student1 = 70;

Student2 = 56;

Student3 = 89;

StudentN = 66;
```

However, because this is very tedious and repetitive, we can create an array that stores students' scores.

```
Scores = [70, 56, 89, 66···score(n)];
```

Although this is not how we declare arrays, you can see it's a lot easier, cleaner, and better than the first method.

Defining an Array

Like all variables, we need to define an array before we can use it.

The best way to do this is to use the variable dollar notation, then the @, parenthesis, and the values we want to store in the array. Consider the example shown below:

```
PS C:\Users\salem> $student_score = @(70, 56, 89, 66)
PS C:\Users\salem> $student_score
70
56
89
66
```

Once we declare and assign values to an array, we get the values stored in the specified array. PowerShell displays each element—an element is each value in an array—in a new line.

We are going to learn how to access each element in an array soon:

Accessing Array Elements

Let us discuss how to access individual elements in an array.

When we want to access an array's element, we use the array's name, followed by a square bracket pair. Inside the square brackets, we pass the index of the element we want to access. An index is the location or number of elements we want to access.

Indexing in PowerShell starts at zero. That means the first element in an array is index 0. Example:

```
PS C:\Users\salem> $student_score[0]
```

70

Therefore, the last element in an array is in the index of the total number of elements – 1.

Try and get the last student score.

To do this, we use the $student_score variable followed by the last index, which is given by 4 – 1. (Total elements - 1)

```
PS C:\Users\salem> $student_score[3]
```

66

If you access an index that does not exist in the array, PowerShell will return an `OperationStopped` **Error**. Here's an example:

```
PS C:\Users\salem> $student_score[4]

OperationStopped: Index was outside the bounds of the array.
```

PowerShell also allows you to select a range of elements within an array. Say, for example, between the first and third score. Here's an example of how we can do this:

```
PS C:\Users\salem> $student_score[0..2]

70

56

89
```

Modifying Array Element Values

Apart from reading an array's elements values, we can use methods provided by the `System.Array` class from .NET framework.

For example, if we want to update the second score in the array, we use the equals (=) notation, which, as you can recall, is a simpler way of `Set-Value` cmdlet.

```
PS C:\Users\salem> $student_score[2] = 98

PS C:\Users\salem> $student_score

70

56

98

66
```

If we access the array's elements, we see that the third value gets updated from 89 to 98. Modifying an array is an incredible functionality as you Script more in PowerShell.

Adding Elements to an Array.

Let us say our classes increases, and we need to add a score for another student. We can do this by using the + operator. Here's an example:

```
PS C:\Users\salem> $student_score = $student_score +
78

PS C:\Users\salem> $student_score

70

56

98

66

78
```

Now we have added a new score to an existing array. Notice how we call the array on both sides of the statement; this is because we are asking PowerShell to interpolate the array variable and then add a new element to it.

You can also use an operator += to append a new element as shown:

```
PS C:\Users\salem> $student_score += 56
PS C:\Users\salem> $student_score
70
56
98
66
78
56
```

NOTE: Arrays have a fixed size, and once created, you cannot modify them in any way. You're probably wondering, "But how were we able to add values?" We will discuss that when talking about ArrayList.

Unfortunately, there is no equivalent of += for removing arrays. It's very hard to manipulate arrays directly in such a manner.

2: ArrayLists

Let us explore a rather peculiar operation that happens in PowerShell arrays. Whenever an element gets added or removed to an array, it creates a new array. Yeap! PowerShell really destroys the existing array and creates a new one.

As you may recall, this is because of arrays' fixed-size characteristics. This function goes unnoticed, especially when working with small-sized arrays. However, if you are working with arrays containing thousands of data, it is clear and easy to identify.

Hence, if you will work with large amounts of dynamic data, you need to forget about Arrays and instead learn how to use ArrayLists for these operations.

ArrayLists are like normal PowerShell arrays. The main difference is that they don't have a fixed size. That means they can dynamically grow or shrink as data grows or shrinks, giving them a higher performance advantage when working with massive amounts of data.

Defining an ArrayList

We define ArrayList the same way we define normal Arrays, but you cast it to `System.Collections.ArrayList` type. Here's an example:

```
PS C:\Users\salem> $student_score =
[System.Collections.ArrayList]@(70, 56, 89, 66)
PS C:\Users\salem> $student_score
70
56
89
66
```

Like an array, elements in the array get displayed in a new line. However, the data type is different. You can view a variable's data type using the `GetType()` method. Here's an example:

```
PS C:\Users\salem> $student_score.GetType()
```

```
IsPublic IsSerial Name                                     BaseType
-------- -------- ----                                     --------
True     True     ArrayList                                System.Object
```

Adding and Removing Elements in ArrayLists

Modifying ArrayLists is different from modifying arrays. To perform these actions, we use the provided ArrayList methods. They `Add()` and `Remove()` methods to add and remove elements in an ArrayList.

To add an element in an ArrayList, use the method shown below:

```
PS C:\Users\salem> $student_score.Add(53)
4
PS C:\Users\salem> $student_score
```

70

56

89

66

53

Once you add an element to the ArrayList, you get a value that shows the added element's index location. Unless in special cases, you will not use this value. To prevent the Add() method from providing the index of a newly added element, assign the value to null. Remember null?

```
PS C:\Users\salem> $null = $student_score.Add(67)
PS C:\Users\salem> $student_score
```

70

56

89

66

53

67

There are ways to negate the PowerShell output, but using $null is best for performance because it's impossible to set its value.

Let us talk about removing elements from an ArrayList.

To do this, we use the Remove() method and pass the value we want to remove to the method.

For example:

```
PS C:\Users\salem> $null = $student_score. Remove(67)
PS C:\Users\salem> $student_score
70
56
89
66
53
```

You can also pass the element's index in the array as shown. However, this is not a very common method when working with large data because it's rare to know the specific data index location.

```
PS C:\Users\salem> $null =
$student_score. Remove($student_score[4])
PS C:\Users\salem> $student_score
70
56
89
```

66

Because of both use cases of Arrays and ArrayList, you will need to choose which is the most efficient data structure to use. Simply put, the larger and dynamic the data, the better it shall be if you go with ArrayList. For smaller and static data, choose Arrays.

3: *Hashtables*

Another core data structure provided by PowerShell is the *hashtable*.

Now Arrays and ArrayLists are very useful when you want to store data with a single index location. However, if you want to correlate data in a single variable, you use a *hashtable,* also called *dictionaries* in other programming languages.

Consider the score ArrayList we have been working with all along. Although we have the data stored, we do not know whose score it is; we can only guess. Using *dictionaries,* we can add a student name.

We express dictionaries in *key-value* pairs instead of indexed locations, which is the case with Arrays and ArrayLists. To get data in the dictionary, you pass PowerShell, the *key,* and it spits out the precise corresponding value.

To declare a dictionary, we use the @ operator, followed by a pair of curly braces. Inside, we pass the key = value data.

Here's an example:

```
PS C:\Users\salem> $student_score = @{Peter = 70; Mary
= 56; Lucy = 89; Miles = 66}

PS C:\Users\salem> $student_score
```

Name	Value
Peter	70
Lucy	89
Mary	56
Miles	66

Boom! Now that's better.

As you can see, each score value corresponds to a specific key pair.

PowerShell dictionaries are unique. Thus, you cannot have duplicate key value pairs. Each unique key has to point to specific value. For example:

```
PS C:\Users\salem> $student_score = @{Peter = 70; Mary
= 56; Lucy = 89; Miles = 66; Peter = 88}

ParserError:

Line |

   1 |  ... t_score = @{Peter = 70; Mary = 56; Lucy =
89; Miles = 66; Peter = 88}

     |
~~~~~
```

| Duplicate keys 'Peter' are not allowed in hash literals.

<u>Reading Values from Hashtables</u>

Since all keys in a dictionary are unique, you can access a value in a dictionary using its key pair.

There're two methods to do that:

1. **Using index like notation:** You can access an element by passing the dictionary's name, followed by the key-value inside square brackets. Here's an example:

```
PS C:\Users\salem> $student_score["Peter"]
70
```

2. **(.) notation:** Another way to access an element using its key is by using the dot (.) notation. Here's an example of that:

```
PS C:\Users\salem> $student_score.Peter
70
```

Either of the above methods works, and it's the dealer's choice—you can choose which you want. Although they have differences, that's a story for another day.

Adding, Updating, and Removing Hashtable Values

There are two main ways to add elements to a Hashtable.

First, we can use the Add() method or create a new index that acts as a unique plus an equal sign to add the elements. Here's an example of both hashtable manipulation methods:

```
PS C:\Users\salem> $student_score.Add('Powell', 92)
PS C:\Users\salem> $student_score
```

Name	Value
Mary	56
Lucy	89
Peter	70
Powell	92
Miles	66

```
PS C:\Users\salem> $student_score
```

Name	Value
Mary	56

Name	Value
Peter	70
Miles	66
Liz	76
Lucy	89
Powell	92

As we have mentioned, dictionaries' key-value pairs must be unique. Therefore, it's good to check for its availability, i.e., check whether a key-value pair exists before you try to allocate a new one.

You can check if a key exists using the `ContainsKey()` method. The method returns a Boolean True if it contains the specified and False if otherwise.

```
PS C:\Users\salem> $student_score.ContainsKey('Liz')
True
```

Once you confirm the existence of a key-value pair in the dictionary, you can reference its key to modify its data as shown:

```
PS C:\Users\salem> $student_score['Liz'] = 67
PS C:\Users\salem> $student_score
```

Name	Value

----	-----
Mary	56
Peter	70
Miles	66
Liz	67
Lucy	89
Powell	92

Unlike adding elements to a dictionary, you can only use the Remove() method to remove elements in an array. Simply pass the key-value pair you want to remove as shown:

```
PS C:\Users\salem> $student_score.Remove('Liz')
PS C:\Users\salem> $student_score
```

Name	Value
----	-----
Mary	56
Peter	70
Miles	66
Lucy	89
Powell	92

Here's a recap of what we've discussed in this section:

Summary

Its no doubt we have covered a lot of information in this section. By now, you should have a good understanding of PowerShell data types such as Integers, Floats, Objects such as Arrays, Dictionaries, and more.

The concepts covered in this chapter are very Fundamental when it comes to programming in PowerShell. I recommend using reading materials and external sources to enhance your understanding of everything we have covered in this PowerShell scripting guide section.

In the next section, we shall cover how to use PowerShell Loops, conditional statements, and Functions:

Section 4

Conditional Statements, Loops, and Functions

As the title suggests, this section shall cover PowerShell scripting and programming features such as conditional statements that allow us to execute a specific code based on conditions, loops, and Functions.

If you're completely new to PowerShell scripting programming—or programming in general—the concepts discussed in this section may seem foreign.

However, if you have some programming familiarity, most of what we shall discuss will be familiar and easy to understand. Either way, the aim is to make these concepts very easy to grasp.

Let's get rolling:

Understanding and Using Conditional Statements

In the previous section about data types, we briefly mentioned Boolean data types, which are binary values that evaluate as either True or False.

In this subsection, we are going to build on Boolean types to construct *conditional statements*.

Let us understand how *conditional statements* work.

How conditional statements work

In PowerShell—and all programming languages supporting them— Conditional statements help run a specific code block if a specific expression—also called a *condition*—evaluates as True. Do not worry about how to express this; we will cover scripting in the next section.

Consider this scenario:

Suppose you want to perform diagnostics on multiple servers using one script. You can start by having the servers' IP addresses. Using conditional statements, you can implement a factor as:

Send ping request to all servers. Are all servers up? Are they all responding? Depending on the response to the above question, yes/no or True/False, we can perform various actions.

Let us discuss how we can use these questions to create expressions.

Comparison Operators

The most common way to build Boolean expressions is by using what we call Comparison operators. We use comparison operators to evaluate between two values and output a Boolean value.

For example:

The expression below is an example of a comparison statement.

```
PS C:\Users\salem> 2 -eq 5
False
```

In this case, the -eq operator checks if the value on the expression's left side is equal to the right side's value. In this case, 2 is not equal to 5, which thus outputs False.

PowerShell supports various comparison operators; they include:

- ‑eq – This operator checks if two values are equivalent, giving a True result if they are.

- ‑ne – This operator is the opposite of the equal operator. It gives a True return if the compared values are not equal.

- ‑gt – The greater than operator compares two values and returns a Boolean True if the value on the expression's left side is higher than the value on its right side.

- ‑ge – This compares two values and returns true when the left side's value is higher than or equal to the right side's value.

- ‑lt – The less-than operator is similar to the0 -ge one but returns true if the left value is less than the right value.

- ‑le- returns true if the left side's value is less than or equal to the right side's value of the set expression.

- ‑contains – used to check if an element is inside the passed variable. For example, if 10 is inside the array @(10, 30, 50, it returns true.

<u>Mental Exercise</u>

Evaluate what the expressions below will return given ($var1 = 54 and $var2 = 7)

$var1 −eq $var2 = ?

$var2 −ne $var1 = ?

$var2 −gt $var1 = ?

$var1 −ge $var2 = ?

$var2 −lt $var1 = ?

$var1 −le $var2 = ?

It is good to note that PowerShell provides more complex comparison operators beyond this book's scope.

Here is a resource link you can use to learn more about them:

https:linkfy.to/tbwXb

Expressions resulting in Boolean values do not have to include variables compared against another. You can also Compare commands and get a Boolean value.

For example:

You can determine if a server responds to ping requests using the Test-Connection followed by a -Quiet parameter. For example:

```
PS C:\Users\salem> Test-Connection google.com -Quiet
```

```
True
```

Having such functionality, we can create *"intelligent"* scripts that perform tasks automatically on our behalf.

Since we have covered the basics of Boolean comparison expression, let us look at conditional statements.

PowerShell *if statement*

The if statement, one of the simplest conditional statements, is useful. Simply, it means: `if a is True, then do b`. The a can be a complex expression, a script, or a command as long the return value is a Boolean.

To define an if statement in PowerShell, we begin with an if keyword, followed by the condition surrounded by a parentheses pair.

Next, we add the code block—the action we want the System to perform when the condition is True—starting with curly braces. The general syntax is as follows:

```
if (condition) {
        # Do these actions

}
```

As you may have seen in the previous code, we use the # sign to indicate a comment. We use comments to document or describe what the code is doing; PowerShell ignores them

Using an if statement, we can explicitly specify what action we want to perform. Consider the code below that displays a message if the server we are testing is online.

```
$my_server = @('157. 240. 3. 35')
if (Test-Connection -ComputerName $my_server[0] -Quiet
-Count 1)

{

    Write-Output -Messsage "$($my_server[0]) is online
"

}
```

-Messsage

freenode. net is online

Using the `Test-Connection` command, we test if a server is online and display a message if True. If false, the program exits.

However, in the real world, you will often need to perform an action that is not true. For example, if the server is offline, we can display a message. We use the else statement to do this.

PowerShell Else Statements

The else statement allows us to add an alternate action the System can perform if a statement's condition evaluates as False. We add the else statement by using the else keyword immediately after closing the if block.

Let us modify the example code above to add a message if the server is offline.

```
$my_server = @("errorserver.com")

if (Test-Connection -ComputerName $my_server[0] -Quiet
-Count 1)

{

    Write-Output -Messsage "$($my_server[0]) is online
"

}

else

{

    Write-Error -Message "$($my_server[0]) is offline"

}

Write-Error: errorserver.com is offline
```

Now, since the server errordomain.com is offline—at least at the time of writing this. I hope no one buys the domain by the time you are reading the book—the program displays an error message, which, as discussed earlier, the Error stream handles.

The concept above is what we call a mutual if/else statement; it works well if you have two mutually exclusive outcomes. In this case: if a server is online, tell me; otherwise, warn me.

Unfortunately, the real world is not that binary:

You will often find more complex situations, including more than ten outcomes at once. For example, a server can be online but not responding to a ping request. A server can also be online, but the DNS does not resolve; it could also be online but using a different port for the service you want to access.

The best way to handle such a real-world case is by using a more complex and evolved conditional statement.

PowerShell if/elseif...else statement

An if/elseif...else statement is a crucial statement that accounts for a wide selection of variability. Think of it as an all-around situation statement. It states:

"If a specific condition is true, do this, else if this happens, do this and do it, again and again, until you handle all variations of situations.

NOTE: It's important that you not confuse these statements with loops!

Consider an example below:

```
$my_server = @("errorserver. com")

if (Test-Connection -ComputerName $my_server[0] -Quiet
-Count 1)

{

    Write-Output -Messsage "$($my_server[0]) is online
"

}

elseif (Test-Connection -ComputerName $my_server[1] -
Quiet -Count)

{

    Write-Error -Message "server does not exist in
the array"

}

elseif (…condition) {

    // do this

}

else {

    // do this if all the above fails
```

}

Not only are we able to handle more situations, but we also add more logic to the code. As you can see, we can chain more than one elseif statement to create a *nested if/elseif...else statement.*

We shall not spend too much time explaining these because they are simple to understand, and their working modality is straightforward.

Practice working with them and use external resources to strengthen your understanding of them:

Control Flow: PowerShell Loops

Programmers have a general rule called DRY. The DRY rule states: ***Don't Repeat Yourself.*** It means you should not write the same piece of code more than once. If you encounter a code appearing more than once, it means you can probably find a way to do it better.

This subsection discusses how to minimize code repetition and uphold the DRY rule using loops.

Before we continue, note that loops are incredibly useful, and once you master them, programming will become like second nature.

However, although they are super important, we cannot discuss all loops within this book's confines. Instead, we shall discuss the most useful ones then provide resources for other PowerShell loops.

Let's take a step back:

Loops defined

Loops are a set of code used to execute a piece of code repeatedly as long a condition evaluates to true. For example, we can say, "as long the server is online, keep downloading Logs every 15 minutes."

Here're the most important loops you should master:

1: The for Loop

A for loop is the most common type of programming loop. We often use it to perform a condition for a specific number of times. The syntax for defining a for loop in PowerShell is as follows:

```
for ($variable_declaration; (condition); iteration) {
```

```
# Execute the following block of code until the
condition is False

}
```

A for loop has four (three?) main parts:

1. **The variable declaration:** Used to define the variable used to check for the condition

2. **Condition:** Specifies the condition evaluated at every iteration of the loop

3. **Increment operation:** The iteration defines the action you want the System to perform after each instance of the loop. For example, it can increase or decrease by 1

A for loop comes in super useful, especially when manipulating Objects such as Arrays, ArrayLists, and dictionaries.

<u>Mental Exercise</u>

Add more values to the $my_server variable and create a for loop that iterates through each of the servers, checking whether each server is online and then displaying the appropriate message.

HINT: Refer to Conditional Statements and PowerShell streams.

2: The While Loop

A while loop is another common type of programming loop. Many programmers consider it one of the easiest loops to implement as it continuously keeps taking action as long as the condition remains true.

Hence: it says, "Do this, while (condition is true)"

For example, consider a loop counter shown below:

```
PS C:\Users\salem> $lcount = 0;

PS C:\Users\salem> while ($lcount -lt 5) {$lcount;
$lcount++}

0

1

2
```

3

4

The loop will continuously execute a piece of code until a condition turns False. It is most useful in cases where a loop's number of iterations is non-predetermined.

Here're some resources to help you learn more about loops:

External Resources

https://linkfy.to/wkxOK

https://linkfy.to/2TXw1

https://linkfy.to/nBYnf

https://linkfy.to/1PisV

Summary

This section has taught you how to use conditional logic to define the handling of a specific condition, control flow to iteration through the code, and perform actions based on each loop.

Although we gave examples, practicing is the only way to master Loops. While that advice is common, it's common for a reason: it works, and it's the best way to become a better computer programmer—using any computer programming language, including PowerShell.

Now let's discuss scripting:

Section 5

Combining Commands and Scripting

To this point, we have been working with standalone commands where we execute the command we want and proceed to the next command.

For simple non-repetitive tasks, this is acceptable. However, that can become very repetitive and tedious when working with large and complex tasks. That's where scripting comes into play.

This section will focus on how to combine more than one command in a single line or save them to an external script that you can then reuse on any supported system.

An example of where chaining commands together can be useful is when working with tasks.

To kill a specific task, you have to make sure it exists, then kill it, using the `Get-Process` command to list the running processes, then using the `Stop-Process` command to kill it.

When it comes to commands, deploying a command once is not an issue, but a hundred times with different computers and processes? That's another ballgame altogether, necessitating scripting.

PowerShell Pipe (|)

One method of combining commands is by using the Pipe feature.

The pipe tool allows you to pass a command's result (output) to another command as an input. We use the *pipe operator* indicated by the symbol (|) – above Enter key to call the pipe.

The general syntax for the pipe operation is:

```
PS > firstCommand | secondCommand
```

The output of the first command gets *piped* into the second command as an input. Once a command gets piped, only the output from the second command gets displayed in the console.

The piping commands method is common among scripting languages such as cmd and bash. In PowerShell, Piping is more interesting than in most other languages because it passes objects instead of strings.

NOTE: Not all commands accept a pipeline input; some will return an error if you pass pipe input.

Piping Objects between Commands

Suppose we wanted to pass the output to the Stop-Process we introduced earlier. In that case, we could use the `Get-Process` to grab the Process ID number first and then pipe that value to the `Stop-Process`.

CAUTION: The example shown below will kill the current PowerShell session.

```
PS C:\Users\salem> Get-Process -Id $PID | Stop-Process
```

The -Id parameters grab the specified process's PID and save it to $PID variable. The variable then gets piped to Stop-Process, which terminates the process.

Piping Arrays Between Commands

PowerShell also allows you to pipe an array of values to a specific command. For example, suppose you have a process you would like to stop at the same instance.

First, you can grab their process IDs and then pipe the array of PIDs to Stop-Process, as shown below:

```
PS C:\Users\salem> $processid = Get-Process notepad,
chrome, explorer | select -expand id
```

```
PS C:\Users\salem> stop-process $processid
```

PowerShell piping can support numerous commands as long as they accept input from pipe commands. However, do not pipe more than five commands in a row. When you want to do so, there's a better way of approaching the issue.

PowerShell Parameter Binding

Let us look at what happens when you pass a parameter to a PowerShell command.

Once a command gets called with a parameter, PowerShell automatically initiates a process called *parameter binding*. The *parameter binding* process matches each object passed to a list of known parameters pre-defined by the command's developer.

Parameters get defined by cmdlets creators, whether that's Microsoft or individual scripters. Hence, if you look at the source code of a command such as Get-Process, you will find a parameter defined as -Id or such. Piping support also gets defined in the PowerShell code. If you pipe information that does not support it, you will get an error.

When you execute a command that does not have a defined parameter—meaning the binding process does not find an appropriate binding—you will get an error as below:

```
PS C:\Users\salem> 'processname' | Get-Process

Get-Process: The input object cannot be bound to any
parameters for the command either because the command
does not take pipeline input...

-----------------output truncated-----
```

You will see that the command does not accept pipeline input. You can check pipeline support for a specific command by using the Get-Help command and -Full parameter.

Again, exploring and practicing is the best way to master these!

PowerShell Scripting

PowerShell scripting is the process scripters use to write PowerShell code in a file and save it for later use.

These scripts store PowerShell code, including loops, arrays, and such. You can think of them as a standalone program that performs a specific action.

For example:

It can be a script that performs diagnostics on IIS servers, a script to perform automatic OS installation, perform backups, and more.

Scripts are nothing special, nor do they offer extra functionality that you cannot perform on the console. However, they allow you to aggregate the commands and create tools you—and others—can use and edit later.

Execution Policy

Before we can start writing PowerShell scripts, we need to allow PowerShell to run them explicitly. By default, PowerShell does not allow script execution as malicious tools can cause real damage to the System.

The Execution Policy that governs the System's security manages the rules for running scripts in PowerShell.

The Execution Policy has four main configuration modes:

1. **Restricted Mode:** This is the default configuration mode that disables the execution of any external scripts

2. **Unrestricted Mode**: This allows you to execute any PowerShell script

3. **AllSigned Mode:** This allows you to run only external scripts that have a cryptographic signature from a trusted source

4. **RemoteSigned Mode:** This mode allows the execution of scripts you write or download from external sources as long as they contain a trusted party signature.

You can view a machine's Execution Policy by calling the `Get-ExecutionPolicy` **command:**

```
PS C:\Users\salem\Documents> Get-ExecutionPolicy

RemoteSigned
```

Or

```
PS C:\Users\salem> Get-ExecutionPolicy

Restricted
```

If you installed PowerShell as shown in the first section, the chances are high that you have RemoteSigned mode enabled. However, if you have Restricted, you can change it to run external scripts.

Use the command:

```
PS C:\Windows\System32> Set-ExecutionPolicy -
ExecutionPolicy RemoteSigned
```

You will need to run PowerShell as an administrator to change the Execution Policy. Confirm the ExecutionPolicy by executing the Get-Execution command.

NOTE: You do not need to change the Execution Policy every time you run PowerShell. The mode gets preserved until explicitly changed by the user.

PowerShell Script Cryptographic Signing

Although I will not dive deep into how the script signing process works, I will briefly mention it.

A cryptographic script signature is an encrypted piece of string appended at the end of a PowerShell script as a comment. Script signatures get created by certificates installed on the device.

These certificates allow you to run scripts when Execution Policy modes are on either AllSigned or RemoteSigned. If a script lacks a properly-signed certificate from a trusted party, PowerShell will block the execution. You can view a signature of a script using the Get-AuthenticodeSignature command.

```
PS C:\Program Files
(x86)\WindowsPowerShell\Modules\Pester\3.4.0\Examples\
Calculator> Get-AuthenticodeSignature .\Add-
Numbers.ps1
```

```
    Directory: C:\Program Files
(x86)\WindowsPowerShell\Modules\Pester\3.4.0\Examples\
Calculator


SignerCertificate                                   Status
StatusMessage              Path
-----------------                                   ------
-------------              ----

A4341B9FD50FB9964283220A36A1EF6F6FAA7840  Valid
Signature verified.        Add-Numbers.ps1
```

For security, always ensure to sign your scripts. You can learn more about how to create signatures from the following resource pages:

https://linkfy.to/5sRA1

https://linkfy.to/7SKoz

https://linkfy.to/FQ4Ik

Writing PowerShell Scripts

Since we've solved the limitations adherent to the PowerShell execution policy, we can start writing executing PowerShell scripts.

You can write PowerShell scripts in any text editor you prefer, whether Sublime, VScode, Notepad++, etc. By default, PowerShell ISE—PowerShell Integrated Scripting Environment— comes installed on most Systems, and you can use that.

However, it has become deprecated, and most programmers don't love it. I recommend using Visual Studio Code with the PowerShell extension installed.

https://code.visualstudio.com

Using PowerShell ISE

You can launch the PowerShell ISE from the start menu or running the command `powershell_ise` from the console.

Doing that will launch an interactive PowerShell environment such as the one shown below:

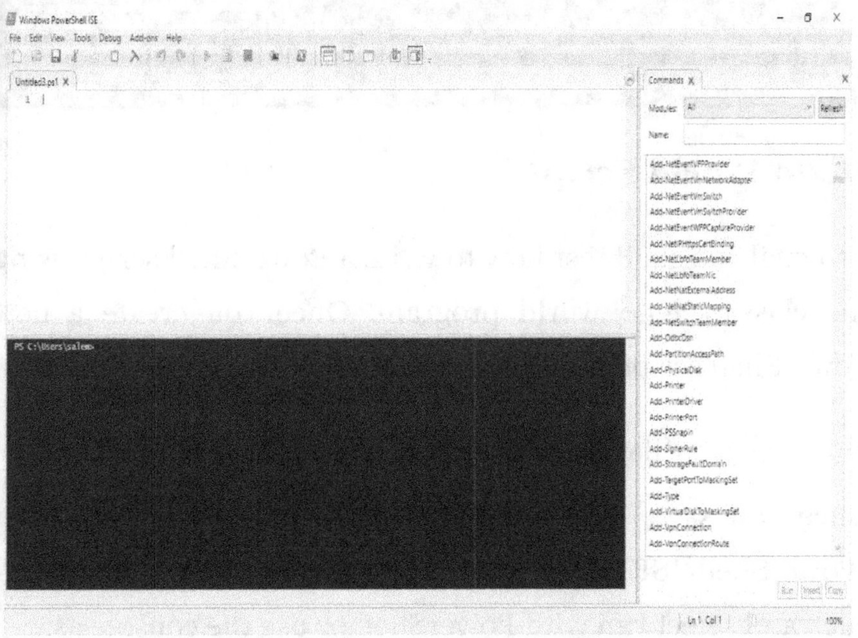

By default, it will create a file called Untitle1.ps1. You can also create a new one by clicking File -> New or press CTRL + N

You can save a script by clicking on File -> Save or CTRL + S, then giving the script a name. Ensure the File has a ps1 extension.

If you are using any other text editor apart from PowerShell ISE, you will need to specify the file type.

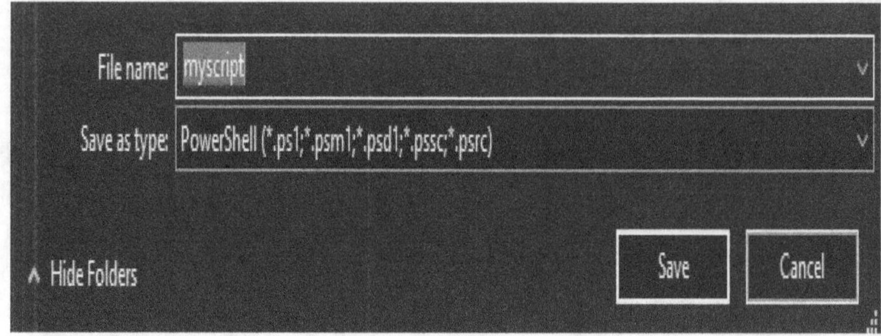

Hello World Script

As usual, we shall test how to write a PowerShell script using the classic Hello world program. Once you create a new PowerShell script and save, write the following code.

```
Write-Host "Hello, world!" ;
```

Once you save, click on the Green icon in the menu bar (PowerShell ISE). For other scripts, you can simply right-click and select run with PowerShell or use the console as:

```
PS C:\Users\salem\Documents> .\myscript.ps1
```

```
Hello, world!
```

Cheers, you have successfully created your first PowerShell script. It may not look like much at the moment, but it's a great place to start.

Using external scripts, you can have hundreds or thousands of lines of code. Once you combine all the skills we have covered in this book, you can create PowerShell scripts and amazing tools.

Conclusion

Without a doubt, there's a ton more we have left uncovered about PowerShell, but as a beginner, what we have discussed is more than enough to get you started on the path to mastering Powershell scripting.

My rallying call to you is to encourage you to think of ways to use PowerShell to automate any repetitive tasks on your machine. Also, use external resources to build on what you have learned from this book.

In parting, remember to have fun; after all, *"Genius is Intelligence having fun!"*

www.ingramcontent.com/pod-product-compliance
Lightning Source LLC
Chambersburg PA
CBHW072059150726
47999CB00005B/1814